Pimp Player Preacher

My Life of Gangs Guns Drugs and God

Ralph W. Hawthorne

Kindle Direct Publishing

Contents

This writing is being released on February 9th; your birthday......
is dedicated to my friend and brother Willie BB Leavy RIP, who,
through thick and thin, the right and wrongs, the good and the bad.
I will always remember you; my greatest wish is that you would
have come to know my Lord and Savior, Jesus Christ, along with
me and served Him with the same time and energy that we utilized
traveling the country but to win souls for Him.

Chapter 1

Police Report (excerpt)

I heard Ralph tell........... That someone wanted to talk to her......... stated that they ignored them and continued walking to the exit she states at this time a black male who she identified as Dale was standing by the doorway .... stated she heard him say b******* you going with me at this time .... stepped up and told him that no one was going with him and observed him reach to the rear of his hips near the rear back pocket and pulled out a small caliber silver handgun .... states that she is not sure if he pulled the gun from his right or left hip area. She described the weapon as a silver metal gun with a white handle, she states that the weapon was a 22 or 25 caliber, she further states she has seen enough handguns to be able to determine the approximate caliber. She was however unable to say whether it was a revolver or semi automatic after seeing Dale pull the gun and hear .... make her objection .... stated that Ralph was pointing his weapon at her and other people in the immediate area.

Chapter 2

The Beginning

Before I get ahead of myself, let's look at how an innocent young kid grew up to find himself in the above situation As a small child, my family moved to Rockford, Illinois from Louisville, Mississippi with no more than the clothes on our backs. The Sledge family of Rockford took us in until my mother could find a place of our own. She and my father were on and off again and he would see her when he would come into town from Chicago. My mom moved into a small house on Lexington Street that was owned by the Sledges. After moving from there we lived in several different apartments, but I can remember the house we moved into on Mulberry Street the most fondly. My mother met a hard-working man named Richard Lewis, and he became our stepfather. At 821 Mulberry Street, they rented the upper and lower apartments where they would occupy the upstairs, and my five brothers and sister were downstairs. My baby brother and sister were born around that time. We had a lot of time to ourselves to allow our young minds to wander.

Some of my best friends at the time were Vincent Brown who moved into the neighborhood from Hawaii. John Wilkins, Johnny Boy Morgan, Kenny and Brian Jarret, Wayne Douglas, Frankie, Charles, Terry, and Mark Freeman, Overtis and Otto Patterson, and Eddie Taylor, to name a few. After walking to Franklin school in the heat, rain, sleet, or snow, we would meet up at one another houses and hang out. We all formed the Mulberry Street gang and the Elm street gang. We would have played wars with wooden swords. I, of course, was with the Mulberry Street gang, and we had a clear view of them from atop the garage on the side rear of our house. When they came to attack, we would peel the tiles off the roof and fly them at them. We had garbage can lids for shields for that reason. That was all fun and games; we would soon afterward get together and go swinging on the big tree. The big tree was at the lil park; the lil park was where the Salvation Army on Kilburn is now. The tree sat on a hill, and we would throw a rope around its huge oak limbs and take off running from one side of the tree, then swing down into the lil park and back up to the other side. We were so creative in making things happen to have fun.

Some of my friends came from off Horseman Street Hal Walker, Pee Wee Ellis, Philip Jamerson, and Bobby Dupree, and they were all from the north side. And Scoopy, who was from Loves Park, he was with us every day. One day while hanging out by the creek, where we would go to sneak and watch some of the young adults hide in a special camp by the creek and sniff glue out of a paper bag, sometimes we would wait until they were done and throw the bag down, and we would go over and pick them up and puff in them, it was the start of my chemical dependency though I didn't realize it at the time. I was so preoccupied with them sniffing that I did not see the dead body in the creek with its legs hanging out, but his head and torso completely submerged. That was the first time I had seen a dead body.

I spent a lot of time in Fairgrounds Park and around the pool because we couldn't go swimming. After all, it cost. So as a youngster, we all swam in the creek. We spent a lot of time at the creek catching crawfish and frying the tails. There was an old, abandoned factory where Fairgrounds Valley Housing stands today that we explored and would find large sheets of cork and use them to float down the creek, trying to knock each other off. We had a lot of fun growing up; those were bonds we all have that have lasted a lifetime. There were train tracks next to the old factory, which is currently dividing the Fairgrounds Valley Housing projects. We would wait for the train to come and hop on it just for the thrills. Later, when we became teenagers, we would hop on the train and ride it to the south side to see the girls. Fairgrounds Park was the place everyone in town would come to after work and school, and the park would be full of people surrounding the basketball courts, where occasionally, there would be fist fights to break out that turned into big brawls. Of course, many girls were always in the park and at the pool where bid whisk, spades, and chess would be played daily. People would come from the east, west, south, and west end. My brother Robert and others became the gatekeepers for the north side and organized the "North Side Soul Takers" a gang of mostly teenagers and young adults who began to hold it down and protect the North side's interest.

Chapter 3

GROWING UP IN THE HOOD

All of this was before the Fairground's housing development was built which is significant because when it was built there were a lot of other brothers and sisters that moved into the hood. To name a few Michael Lewis, Sonny Partee, Lil Parker, Mark Harris, Eddie and Chuckie Laster, Wayne, Chuckie, Lop, and Bae Bae Richardson whose father James B was a notorious player; James B was a prolific crap-shooter and spent a lot of time grooming the fellas on how to get money.

My brother Robert was a key leader "the north side soul takers" nobody could come into the neighborhood without the risk of being robbed or hurt. It did not take me long to find myself getting into mischief, at the age of 9 years old I took up stealing things like purses, bicycles, etc. and because the house next door from us was a bootleg house where they sold illegal alcohol and pimps and prostitutes worked from there, it didn't take me long to get a glimpse of the GAME. Most of those that I saw driving flashy cars were pimps' bootleggers players and street hustlers. I remember thinking that that's how poor people became successful, so I began to listen in on their conversations. one of my first hustles I would build a shoe shine box and shine the player's shoes in the neighborhood and listen to them spit game at each other and " talk streets" so, by the time I was about10 years old I was arrested for my first time, I stole a lady's purse at the laundry mat and got caught. I ended up in juvenile detention, it was the start of many incarcerations as a juvenile offender, including robbery, car theft, theft of property, and arson. Juvenile detention became a regular occasion in my young life. My friends and I would often steal cars just to joyride and we would wreck the cars just for the fun of it all. Myself, Philip Jamerson, Calvin Heath, Greg Mannery, and Robert Wheeler were the usual suspects. We would drive at extremely reckless speeds in the city and on the back roads sometimes topping over one hundred miles per hour.

One night we stole a car, it was Scoopy, Michael Lewis, myself, and Robert Wheeler, someone spotted their car and started chasing us. We sped through the streets of Rockford until we found a spot to bail out. We had all agreed that in the case that something like this happens we would make it to the party that was going on. I made it to the party but Mike and Scoopy and Robert never showed up. Late that night Mike called my house, and my mother gave me the phone. Mike then told me that Scoopy had fallen on the ice, hit his head, and begun to bleed out of his mouth and nose. Scoopy died that night, and I was devastated. We were 14 years old. It turned out that he had died from a brain aneurysm.

Chapter 4

CLOSER THAN A BROTHER

My brother David is not only my brother, but he was also my partner in crime. We used to create fake petitions to go door to door to find out if people were at home, and if we got no answer, we would get their names off their mailboxes and look for their phone numbers in the phone book and call their home, if no answer, we would break in. We would keep a pocket full of money from all the property we would sell to the known fences. Those were the fun days for us until David got caught and was sent away to the department of corrections, the Illinois youth commission., I began to intensify my activities in the streets, I felt so ahead of the time, so I would hang out with the older guys and became known to be fearless, and I wasn't afraid to take risks of any kind. Me and one of my childhood friends, Martin did an armed robbery of a weed spot once. I remember feeling the adrenaline rush of having the power to move people at my command. That was the first armed robbery I did of many. Being a young man with money in my pocket, the product to sell and buy the clothes and things that my heart desired was exciting as well. I had dropped out of high school by now and had a lot of time on my hands to become creative as to how to get my next buck. It wasn't long before I ended up back in Juvenile detention. one day, while in solitary confinement, I set the mattress on fire in my cell and was charged with arson and as a result, they marched me next door to the adult county jail where I was kept until they sent me to IYC "The Illinois Youth Commission" A maximum security facility for boys in Joliet Illinois where I befriended several young men who were gangster disciples. I quickly learned the creeds and laws of the mob, but I stayed on the fringes and out of the way.

One day we planned a takeover of our entire cell block so we breached the control center, what began as an idea to breach the control center turned into a full-scale riot, other cell blocks were opened, and different gang factions began to fight and demolish the facilities, guards were being beaten and stomped as fights were happening all over. I and two other guys were able to "make the fence" and get away. We didn't know where we were going or even how to get there. State police were searching all over for us, we were eventually caught in a cornfield and returned to the institution. A few others and I were stripped down to our underwear and detained in cells in vacant cell houses that didn't have any windows. Mosquitos were my greatest enemy We had no mattresses or blankets. I either slept on the cold hard steel or the cold hard floor. I was fed through a space under the door where the plastic food tray was slid into the room. After about two weeks I was given clothes and interviewed before being returned to the population, but in the interview, I started reading out loud what he was writing, and he was astonished that I was able to read his writing upside down, so as a result, even though most of the guys involved were shipped out to more secure facilities they chose to send me to Valley View in Elgin Illinois which had a school and was an educational institution I studied and kept out of trouble

Shortly after being paroled out of St. Charles a maximum-security facility that one had to go to for parole hearings. I started back with my illegal activities; burglary became my choice of hustle along with selling pills.

Hittin A Lick

One day myself and my Lil brother Mark Freeman was standing in front of the grocery store on West State Street when I peered into the window and observed a woman at the counter gently pulling bills out of her purse as if she was peeling the bills from a large roll of other bills. We waited until she came out of the store and began to put her groceries into her car all while leaving her purse in the shopping cart. I timed her so that when she turned her back to put more groceries in her car, I ran as fast as I could and snatched the purse out of the grocery cart, and ran through the parking lot with Mark running right alongside me until we got to his mother's house where we entered the side door and down into the basement.

When I dumped the purse out on the floor a large amount of money fell out. It appeared to be proceeds from a business of some sort. The next morning, I set out to find a car to purchase, I went to Humphrey Cadillac and Oldsmobile where I spotted this beautiful 1963 white Cadillac sedan, I purchased it on the spot, and afterward, I equipped it with a television and antenna, sound system, fog lights, and gangster white walls, I was 17 years old and the envy of the city, but I also once again caught the attention of law enforcement.

Chapter 5

ALL AS ONE

Some of the older gangsters, Lonnie "Son the Don" Eason, Pete Nitti, Ginn, Kenny Tito, Rayfield, BB, and a few others, including Ronnie Fort, and Bradley Baker had now gotten out of the penitentiary and were calling a GD (Gangster Disciple), BD (Black Disciple) meeting to organize in Rockford at the Valerie Percy Apartments which became headquarters for the mob. D City a clubhouse in the basement of one of the apartment buildings, was the meeting location when we were not partying. GDS and BDs became "all as one" and all of us from the North Side aligned with the mob. I was still a shorty and was asked to oversee all the shorties in the mob. I was equipped with a 45-caliber handgun and was given the authority to call all shots, especially the North side. I was very reluctant because even at an early age, I wasn't into anybody telling me what to do, and I knew that the position came with responsibility and with that accountability, so I sat on the decision and left town for a couple of weeks to stay with my godmother in Battle Creek Michigan.

When I returned, everything had cooled down, and the mob had moved on to other things like extortion of drug dealers and pimps, armed robberies, etc.

I too had moved on and rather than follow the brothers down that path, I resorted to once again burglarizing. In February of that year, I was arrested again for multiple counts of residential burglary I was sentenced to 1 year in the county jail and 5 years on probation. I ended the year term on work release after my probation officer helped me secure a job with the City of Rockford Sewer Department. I was doing good and staying out of trouble I moved out of my mom's basement at 18 and rented my first-ever apartment on my own. I was on my way to living a crime-free and respectful life that is until I started buying weed by the pound from an Italian guy on the job. I started selling weed from my new spot after I got off work until I started making more money selling weed than what the job was paying me. My weed customers were gamblers too, so every night I would open my apartment up as a crap house and cut the game and make more money.

Through my newfound hustles, I bought a white Lincoln Continental with suicide doors and was back in the mix. money was coming so fast and heavy that I put three of my neighborhood shorties on the count and armed them with handguns and they protected me and my interest.

Chapter 6

GLOWING

My game was getting so tight that everywhere I went at least one of my guys was always with me. Mark Freeman was a family friend and just like my little brother. Our mothers were like sisters to each other and when they went out to party together, we would all stay either at Ms. Viola's house or at our house. I was heartbroken when he caught a murder case and was sentenced to thirty years. Thank God he's out of prison and doing well for himself.

I was living the high life with nice cars nice clothes wonderful place to live with females all around me trying to get with me I had a lot of respect on the street but had not forgotten choosing fees that were in effect.

Every day different females were showing up at my apartment. I was in such high demand and was making so much money that I quit the job and went back to hustling. One female that caught my attention was Mary Jane I came to realize that she was the baby mama of a guy I had been hunting that had broken into my apartment and stolen a gun and money from me. We began to get familiar with one another, she was a hard-working young lady caring for her two young daughters. Though she lived in the housing developments, she was good-looking and well-kept. As we got to know one another I shut the crap house down and stopped selling weed and moved in with her and once again tried to go on the straight and narrow.

Myself, BB, and Bradley used to get together every weekend though to find where the crap house was to gamble. One night, Bradley came by my house with his brother Bruce to get with me to go gambling. I wasn't home at the time, so they went without me. Bradley got killed that night at the crap house in an argument with a man over a bet. When I found out about it. I went over to the scene, and I soon found out that not only did Bradley get killed but the fella that shot him twice in the head had been killed by Bruce after the fella shot Bradley. Bruce was charged with murder and ended up going to the penitentiary even though in my opinion his crime was an act of passion. I attempted to contact BB the entire night to inform him that Bradley had gotten killed but couldn't he didn't show up until the next day. We were all devastated, Bradley was a good brother with a unique sense of humor and was fun to be around.

Chapter 7

Going Straight

I got a job at the newly opened mall called Cherryvale at a men's clothing store called Don Di Fashions. Because I was well known, I began to sell and dress a sizable portion of the Rockford Illinois and surrounding areas Black community and my wardrobe was one of the best in the region amongst players.

Rockford Illinois was THAT SPOT the town we grew up in is a long way from what they're growing up in now. So many Black-owned businesses when we grew up, you can't even name 'em all. Iceberg Slim, the original Monkey D, Fast Eddie, High Pockets, & Pretty Bob James B, Lee Jay, Eddie, and Chuckie just to name a few of the Legends that stomped these grounds.

Eldorado, Tuxedo, Jazz bah, Vee Hi, Idle Inn & Zodiac were all Black Clubs. Not to even mention the bucket of blood Rock Tap. We lived through the absolute best of Rockford. It will never be the same.

There were codes and ethics to the game that most players lived by. There was a sense of honor among thieves. A man's word was his bond rather it was among players, pimps, or gangsters. Be-

tween 1975 and early 1979 I went from salesperson to assistant
manager to store manager.

I started snorting cocaine and drinking what we call top-shelf
alcohol, cocaine was a social drug at the time and almost everyone
I knew at the mall was casually using it. We would on occasion do
each other favors and cop/buy for each other from our connections.
It was a normal occasion to visit someone else's store and they
would be using in the back room and willing to turn you on.

Getting Caught Up

One day Betty from one of the restaurants at the mall recommend-
ed a fellow by the name of Scott to work for me, well I interviewed
him and he seemed to be a pretty likable guy he was a fast talker so
I decided to go ahead and hire-him, well he joined in with us with
the partying and the weed and snorting cocaine all became a norm,
so one day he asked me to cop some cocaine for him as a favor as we
all had done for each other. I did it and so I went to his house after
work to drop it off and we set there we talked and we laughed and
we shared stories and we snorted cocaine and the phone started
ringing. I didn't think anything of it, I just thought they must be
pretty busy but it just kept ringing and he kept answering it and
after a while, I started telling him about my background and how
I was working the job trying to work my way off of probation for
the burglary charge that I had against me and after a while he got
very quiet and he looked me in my eyes and he just said "Ralph I
can't do this to you "and I was like what? and he said "the phone
is ringing Ralph cause this is a setup, he said I work for the IBI the
Illinois Bureau of Investigation and we were investigating you for
selling drugs but I know that you're not a drug dealer I know that

you are only doing this for friends" and I just can't do this to you I can't see you take this fall like this with all that you have to lose and I freaked out, I didn't know what to do and ultimately I ended up leaving that place

I began to remember how Scott had just come from out of nowhere and how Betty had explained to us that he was traveling through Rockford and that he was a truck driver, and his truck broke down in Rockford. For whatever reason, he decided to stay there so that was the story. I got out of there by the skinny skin of my teeth and they started calling the store and asking me to at least turn the money in and just give the money back and you know I was like what money? I was like I did not know what you are talking about and so that was one of those situations where I was truly fortunate that I did not end up catching a delivery a drug conspiracy or a delivery charge, so I thank God for that.

Chapter 8

Just Can't Stop

In 1978 I left the job and started hustling again. I got in the box and started selling cocaine around that time; one of my old friends, BB got out of prison. I gave half of my product to him and gave him a part of my wardrobe, and we started off hustling together; we would make the drug runs to Chicago, and our customers would be waiting for us when we got back. So much money, material possessions, guns, jewelry, clothes, etc. came in. It was at that time that I caught my first hooker, Slim was a young dark-skinned, short, good-looking girl with the ambition to see me further my enterprise, so I took her to school as to what I expected from her (the law) and how I expected for her to abide by my every rule. She was game, and so I put her down on the track (hoe stroll). My first night's trap (pay, choosing fee) was incredibly attractive and added handsomely to what I had made selling cocaine that day. She worked for me as my main Hooker for four years. That was the start of a lengthy journey of pimping, drug dealing, drug, and alcohol use, sticking up, and gun plays. BB produced a snowball (white girl) shortly afterward. He says he pulled her right from her job at Burger King; he put her down with my girl that night. That was the beginning of a relationship; he and I was as close as my brothers. Where you saw me, you saw him. We were dressed to impress always.

It wasn't long afterward, while shopping at the Merry-Go-Round at the mall, I caught the attention of a young Italian girl whom I called Star; she immediately made it clear that she was interested in me. I picked her up after her shift, and just like that, she became my second hooker; I was now double-breasted with salt and pepper. She and my main girl got along perfectly, and she went to work for me that night, but things don't always go smooth sailing. I found out that her family had a history with the mafia, and before long, her brothers and others were hunting me.

BB and I were like vampires working the girls on S. Main at night as we spent time together at the local bars Jazz Bah, the legend, Elks, and Tuxedo club. Always on the prowl for a new game (girls). One night while out til daylight, another player asked me to let him and his girl crash at my place and get some rest. As a result of my saying yes, I started hearing that the police were looking for me. As it turned out, the girl he had was underage, and the player and I were wanted for pimping and pandering I then had to go underground, which meant that I had to stop selling and lay low.

Chapter 9

Everything That Shines Ain't Gold

As stated before everything doesn't always stay calm and smooth sailing. News started to circulate that a trick was found shot to death in a vehicle close to the hoe stroll. Detectives quickly ruled it a homicide related to prostitution, and they started putting a lot of pressure on the girls on the street for information. BB informed me that it was his girl that had accidentally shot the trick and it was eating at her, so we packed up and moved our operations to Madison, Wisconsin. Now out from under the scrutiny of the Rockford police department, we set out to break into our fresh territory. I was still being sought for the pimping and pandering case when I got word that BB had been arrested for a parole violation while back in Rockford and his girl had confessed to the murder. In her confession, she attempted to implicate me and BB, so now they were searching for me for questioning of the murder. BB was released and joined me in Madison. Star had gone back home to her family and Slim had gone missing it turned out that she had gotten with another pimp and left town.

one night I went to a gambling house and immediately walked to my left there was a door open, and there was another player passed out in the bed all of his hookers were knocked out of sleep as well. I noticed that his pants were in the middle of the floor, so I stepped in, checked his pants, and came up with a huge knot of money. I didn't know how much it was, but I stuffed it in my pocket and asked one of my partners to give me a ride to the hotel where I was staying. I walked into the room, pulled the wad out of my pocket, and it was a jackpot, nothing but $100 bills so just like that, I was back in the mix again. I decided that I needed to get away from Rockford and the heat of everything so I jumped a plane at greater Rockford airport and went to Memphis, TN to visit a friend; it's there that I bought a nice white Lincoln Continental, it was beautiful triple white, and I called BB who had gotten out jail, and I flew him down to Memphis, we drove the Continental back to Rockford. By the time I got back to Rockford, I heard that Slim was back in town so I went and found her and charged her up she agreed that she owed me, so we hit the road, we traveled from one state to the other from Rockford all the way to Los Angeles, San Diego California and then to Vegas it was now 1981. I had located one of my childhood friends Mike who was living in Los Angeles so him, myself my girl and his girl decided to go to Denver, Colorado we were passing through Las Vegas where I lost my entire bankroll shooting craps even before we had settled into a room, eaten or anything. I spent the next nine months trying to win my money back. Mike decided to strike out and head to Denver with his girl and had intentions of returning to Vegas,

Chapter 10

THE VEGAS STRIP

My girl and I stayed in Vegas, and she worked the streets of the Vegas Strip and downtown on Fremont St. Those were the times when the hotels had keys on a tag with the room number on it. I had one and she had one. One day I came to the room and once I walked in immediately two men came in the room behind me, they had access with a key. They were plain clothes, vice police that had busted my girl and had the room key. They were very unseemly-looking guys, they put me in handcuffs and began to walk me to their car. It was a small Camaro and when we reached the car door some people began to pile out of the motel room directly in front of where they were parked. They looked at each other and began to take the handcuffs off me and said to me.... "Consider yourself to be lucky." Once again, luck had struck my side. I later found out that the two police officers had been rumored to murder pimps and leave their bodies in the mountains of Las Vegas. Whew!

After I hadn't heard from Mike for a few weeks I attempted to reach him at his mother's house in Los Angeles. When his mother answered the phone, she informed me that my mother had passed away in Illinois and my family had been searching for me. I called home and was told that she had been buried the day before. I was devastated, Mike came back to Vegas and from there we headed to Madison Wisconsin but against my better judgment I drove down to Rockford one night while my girls were working, and I ended up getting arrested for the pimping and pandering case. I stayed in jail for a couple of weeks until my preliminary hearing at which time the witnesses refused to testify, and I was released. Before heading back to Madison, I encountered a high-yellow, red-bone girl whom I named Red. Red chose me and the money was good, these were what I called through bread veterans in the game and was dedicated hoes. The name of the game was whatever it took to keep our hustle alive. Me and BB went on a mission one day where we recognized a robbery opportunity so without delay, we gunned up and headed toward our target. I took the lead and approached the target and announced that "this is a robbery don't make it a murder" the gentleman had another guy there in the adjacent vehicle as we stepped between the two vehicles I reached for the proceeds and the shooting started. It suddenly felt like fire in my hand and dropped the proceeds at which time we backed out in a blaze of gunfire, as we ran down the street, I realized that it was BB that had shot me in my hand, I was bleeding fervently. We arrived at a BB'S snowballs house where she was able to bandage me up, it was an enter and exit wound of my left thumb. I thought about how lucky I was that it didn't turn out worse.

Other episodes could have ended in disaster as well. Back in Madison, we went on a mission to stick up a dope house. What we didn't know was that the door was fortified like Fort Knox as we kicked and kicked it would not budge so we started firing into the door. The element of surprise was one of the most crucial factors when it came to sticking up. We had lost our advantage and had to retreat. I thought about how we could have been met with gunfire and how lucky we were.

Chapter 11

Close Call

W e decided to take a trip to Minneapolis Minnesota to work the girls and one day as we were all in the motel room after sending the girls to the track. We were interrupted by a big knock on the door. When I looked out the window I looked down and an officer was pointing a shotgun toward the room window. We were ordered to open the door and file out and get down on our bellies. We all obeyed their demands at which time we were handcuffed and informed that they had a report that we had robbed a trick at gunpoint. None of that was true but the scariest part of it all was that there was a pistol in the room. One of the guys had put it in the cushion of one of the chairs and zipped it back up. After a search of the room, we were released from the handcuffs and the officer in charge began to apologize to us, what he didn't know was that he was sitting on a large pistol as he did so. Once again, I thought of how lucky I was that they didn't discover the pistol we could have easily been falsely charged with armed robbery. After spending time in Minnesota, I began to make plans to head out to Montana where some of my homeboys were and reported that the money was good. I had met a brother from Chicago who was single-breasted and wanted to take his game on the road with me, so we partnered up and began to work the girls up through Minnesota and Wisconsin, when we reached Fargo North Dakota the money coming in was so good that we decided to camp out there and work the girls. We were the only black people in the whole town, which was good business for the girls, but it wasn't long before the girls got busted for prostitution. It was at that time that my road dog retrieved a pistol from his baggage and announced that we must get the money to raise the girls from jail. It was my experience that the girls would spend a couple of days in jail before being released. I couldn't tell that to my friend he was insistent on going on a robbery spree. I told him that he was on his own because those girls would do seven days, but we would get seventy years and it wouldn't take much to identify us as we were the only two black guys in the city of which I was aware. He headed out to a convenience store and proceeded to rob it. He took the money in the cash register, robbed the six customers in the store at the time, and took the car keys of one of the customers before moving everyone into a cooler. After returning to the motel room that we shared he talked about bonding his girl out the next morning. I tried to explain that it was a foolish move. Nevertheless, the next morning we loaded up the car and proceeded to exit the parking lot where we were surrounded by police squads and unmarked cars.

They ordered us out of the car at gunpoint and took us to their headquarters where they took pictures of us to show the victims. Though the officers were saying that I fit the description the victims picked him out and he was charged with seven counts of armed robbery, seven counts of kidnapping, and car theft. They released me but confiscated all my money, my car, and all my clothes so there I was on the streets of Fargo with nothing. I was able to send home for money and got a room. One day while hanging out doing nothing a brother approached me... I was so surprised to see him because I thought I was the only black left in the town. As it turned out, Barry had just gotten out of jail. Barry was a short-change artist from NY shortly afterward the girls got out of jail and authorities released my car and belongings we hooked up and left town.

Chapter 12

Canada and More Trouble

From there I decided to head further north into Canada. With Barry in tow and we landed in Winnipeg, Canada. Barry would take my car by the day and return with a bankroll every single day. It was a great partnership. Of course, he paid me every day.

My man BB was incarcerated again but we sent for his girl Dee, who joined us even though she was pregnant and had her and BBs baby in Winnipeg. My girl was getting bank every night while we were there. We were staying on the 16th floor in downtown Winnipeg.

Lucky or Blessed?

One night I came into the apartment and my girl was nervously pacing the floor when I noticed that the dining room table was full of Canadian currency. She had hit a major sting. For some reason, I decided to pack up and leave Winnipeg while my girl stayed behind to continue working the streets of Winnipeg.

Dee had had her baby and had decided to take the drive with me back to Rockford. The very next morning the Canadian mounted police and immigration service raided my apartment and took my girl to jail. I don't know to this day what that was all about, rather it was a setup gone wrong or I was just lucky once again. After she was released, I flew from Chicago to Winnipeg only to be met by customs at the Winnipeg Airport. I was detained overnight and departed back to Chicago, so I then caught a flight from Chicago to Grand Forks N. Dakota, and caught a greyhound bus across the border to Winnipeg. I was back in and on top of my Pimpin.

Chapter 13

Heading Back to Familiar Territory

A fter leaving Winnipeg for the last time my girl and I flew back to Chicago, and we ended up back home in Rockford, where we settled down for a while all while working my girl on the hoe stroll on Horseman Street. It was nowhere near the kind of money coming in from Horseman Street as it was in the major cities that we had explored but it was ok. We spent a lot of time at the hole-in-the-wall of a bar called the Star Tap where all the street hustlers, prostitutes, alcoholics, and drug addicts spent time together regularly.

My brother Robert was so entrenched in the neighborhood that everyone called him the Mayor of Horseman Street.

Hustling there in the neighborhood was grimy but at least I knew everyone, I grew to be complacent. It was there that I first started using cocaine intravenously. The way I figured was that I was highly addicted to snorting and smoking it, which was expensive, and that it would not take as much if I started shooting, so I did. Boy was I wrong, I was now snorting, smoking, and shooting, and then I started speedballing (shooting heroin and cocaine together)

I had fallen off so badly that by this time I was sleeping on Robert's couch and all of mine and my girls' clothes were in garbage bags, and we were hauling them around from pillar to post. I was still getting paid by my girl, but the money was nowhere near where it used to be nor was it enough to keep my habit going. My girl got wind of me shooting and she just stopped working altogether.

Chapter 14

TROUBLE ON EVERY HAND

One cold snowy February night BB and I got a call from Tito who wanted us to ride to Milwaukee with him to retrieve the runaway that had contacted him and wanted to come back to him and wanted him to come and get her. Tito drove from Rockford to Madison where we were celebrating BBs birthday. When Tito showed up, we piled into his car and headed to Milwaukee to the pool hall that the runaway said that she would be at. It was snowing extremely hard, and we were drinking Korbel Brandy along the way. When we finally arrived, BB was passed out in the back seat, and I had one of my girls in the car with us. Tito and I headed up the stairs to the pool hall, but when we walked in, we didn't see the runaway hooker, suddenly she and two other hookers came out of the bathroom. I told Tito that I had spotted her, so he approached her and said, "let's go" at that time, one of the other hookers stepped in between Tito and the runaway at which time, Tito pulled his pistol and smacked her in the face with it, and the pistol flew out of his hand and landed across the room at as we headed to the highway back to Madison. Tito began to take out his anger on the runaway and while I drove, he began to beat her. We were arrested and charged with kidnapping and reckless use of a firearm. While in Jail BB's brother was murdered back in Illinois. When BB got the news, he was escorted to my cell where I was able to try and comfort him. I had never seen him experience so much pain. I could only hold him and tell him that it was going to be all right. He wanted to get his hands on the perpetrator. Thank God he was in jail. We ended up spending only two weeks in jail when once again the victim didn't show up for our preliminary hearing the cases were tossed out of court, and we had to be released.

Three men arrested for abduction, gunplay

Back in Rockford, I so happened to stop by my brother Roberts's place and he and his woman were fighting in the middle of the street. Robert started to beat her badly and a young man known by her family stepped in and tried to pull Robert off her. He and the young man began to fight, and words were exchanged along with threats of physical violence. Robert and I began to ride around in my car and Robert made a few stops to retrieve a weapon. Later that day we were inside the crap house at Robert Bells place when Robert said he was going across the street to the store. We were in the basement when suddenly I heard gunshots. Because we were in a small room in the basement and Robert had gone upstairs to exit, I couldn't see what was going on. When the shooting stopped, I heard someone say.... It's Robert he's been shot! As I made my way to the front of the room Robert was emerging from a side room with a look of shock on his face. I asked him had he been hit, and he said yes and that he thought it was three times. The Paramedics were called, and I joined him in the ambulance.

As it turned out, he had been hit three times, once in the chin and twice in the back. When we retrieved his hat, it had a bullet hole in it. The young man was serious. Robert survived. This was one of many times he had escaped death. In 1996 we lost him to the dreaded disease called AIDS. He was my big brother whom I adored and, in many ways, emulated. He was a lady's man and a prolific hustler. He was a tall dark well-built and bow-legged fella that the girls chased after relentlessly. He was a pimp and a player that just couldn't let go of the monkey on his back called drugs.

After a while, I started smoking crack, and that was when my life became a living hell. It all started when, as a pimp, we would all rendezvous at each other's place of residence after the women were done working for the night and we counted the balance of our proceeds. A young man amongst us introduced us to a new method of preparing cocaine that was called freebasing. That is where we would purchase the powder cocaine from him and he would begin the process by adding baking soda to it, putting it in a vile and adding water, and then putting it into a pot of boiling water until the product began to boil inside the vile. He would then take it out of the pot and rest the vile in ice water and twirl the vile around until the substance began to harden into a rock. That was a new process that few people had seen at that time. We would take a piece of the rock and put it on top of a screen in a glass pipe, heat it with a torch and smoke it. That was the beginning of my crack habit.

The cost was no problem for me at the time because I had women prostituting for me and I was dependant on each of their quotas per night, this was a new way of getting high and so much more intense of a high than snorting but there was no way to measure its impact on my life at that point going forward. I was slowly turning into a monster it was nothing inside me that was good. overtime I lost everything.

Chapter 15

A Bright Light

O ne day I was at a bar on W. State Street and as I was exiting to turn left onto the sidewalk, I encountered three young girls walking up the street toward me. I was struck by one of them so after I let them past me, I called out "Hey! "All three turned around and the one that caught my eye said, "who me." I said "yeah, you" we started talking and she gave me her phone number. I didn't call her so one day I was on West State Street again sitting on the hood of my car when I spotted her walking up the street toward me. I stopped her once again and she asked me why I hadn't called her. I told her that I had lost her number. The truth was, I was tired of living the life and I didn't want to wreck hers but she was persistent in getting with me and I saw her off and, on all the while, still working slim on the streets. Well, it wasn't long before she was pregnant with my very first child. I was 27 years old, and she was eighteen. Granted to say that after a while this combination of difference of age and experience started to run into conflicts. My life was a mess with nowhere to live so she acquired an apartment and we started to live together. Life was incredibly challenging, and the relationship was very conflicting because by this time she too had started snorting cocaine.

Shortly after meeting her me and my man Dixon (may he RIP) was in the bathroom shooting up and when we were done and came out, she was very curious as to what we were doing so I told her. Her following words were, "I want to try that." I immediately became extremely angry and sternly looked at her and said "no, no you don't, and don't you ever ask me that again" then I told her that anybody willing to offer that to her was not her friend. She was taken aback by the tone in my voice, and I hoped that she would never get caught up in the game. She was young and Nieve and had a full life ahead of her. She came from a loving home; her father was a preacher and she had grown up in the church. I saw good qualities in her and thought to myself, that she would make someone a good wife one day but not me. I did not see that level of commitment to her, and I wanted not to see her exposed to my lifestyle. But one's environment speaks sometimes louder than words and she started to get deeper and deeper into cocaine. I did not even want to know if at some point someone in my dope fiend circle had introduced her to shooting or smoking but she never did it around or with me. During it all she had my second child but that did not stop her from getting high and both of our lives were on a slippery slope; she began to prostitute to keep up our habit. These were some of the darkest days of my life by now we had two children that were mine but had had a child early in her teens that lived with his dad's parents. She started to receive public aid and food stamps which we would use to buy or trade for drugs. Our two small children were victims of our neglect for many years. And then there was our third child, I saw nothing good about this situation and was miserable every day of my life even though I had gotten to the point that I would stay up 5,6,7 days at a time getting high and drinking.

I decided to apply for SSI for my addiction and alcohol. I was diagnosed as a chronic drug addict and alcoholic with an anti-social disorder by their appointed Psychiatrist. I two began to get a monthly check and food stamps which all went for drugs and alcohol.

I lost all my credibility and status, and trouble was always not that far away. I was shot once, but by the grace of God, the bullet traveled downward, it entered my jacket at the shoulder, proceeded down my sleeve and grazed my wrist. I was pent down in the middle of the street all while bullets were raining down around me. So close that I felt the concrete splash up onto my face. Bullets were landing all around me and when I was able to make it to my feet they intensified until I found refuge between two houses. I could hear the bullets slamming against the house as I ran toward it. man was I lucky!

Even though I was down and out, BB stopped by to see me one day. He and a group of guys were selling a lot of drugs and making a lot of money, but they were also using a lot. Using to point that all of them were geeking and staying up for days at a time. Living as if there was no tomorrow. One day at the invitation of BB. I visited one of their dope spots in Concord Commons a low-income housing complex. We were getting high, and I noticed a young man sitting on the couch staring at BB and watching his every move. I pulled BB to the side and warned him about what I was observing and that he needed to be careful and watch out for him. He dismissed my warning and continued to carry on, just before I left, I warned him repeatedly, and he dismissed my warnings. A few days later, there was a knock at the door and the person asked for BB. When BB came to the door and stepped outside that's when it happened, twelve shots rang out all hitting BB and killing him. It was the person that I had warned him about that was charged with his murder, it was his very own cousin. That was one time in my life when I realized that if he had survived, I would have told him, "I TOLD YOU!

Chapter 16

Death is Always a Step Away

One day while at the drug house to buy some rocks I bumped into Eddie. Eddie ended up in front of me at the door where they were serving the drugs through a hole. He was talking to the person on the other side of the door when suddenly a gunshot rang out. I did not know where it came from, but it was loud. I took off and down the stairs and when I looked back Eddie was stumbling down the stairs, he had been shot in the chest for no apparent reason. By the time I drove out of the alley and around the front Eddie was sliding down between two cars until he was laying there on the ground, I pulled over and went to assist him. He kept telling me that his legs were cold. Eddie died two days later. Whew! Once again, I was so lucky.

So was the way of the streets. RIP Eddie Finklea

Chapter 17

A Slippery Slope

I was on a slippery slope. Every dime mattered to me at this point, I was at a bar one night and bought a bag of cocaine from a fella I had known most of my life. When I got home to use it, I quickly realized that he had sold me a dummy bag. A bag of cocaine that looked like cocaine but wasn't.

I began to search for him high and low but being a dope fiend himself he knew how to hide in broad daylight like most of us did when we wanted to.

Time went by and I found out that he was selling for a guy on Chestnut Street. I went there and confronted him, and he promised that he would make it right if I came back later. Well, that became a familiar story from him until one day I got fed up and borrowed and long nose thirty-eight revolver from Frankie Freeman and I went in and approached him again. This time he began to talk to me very disrespectfully at which time I backed up from him and pulled the pistol from my waist and demanded that he give me ALL his dope and money. At that time one of the fellas in the house heard the commotion looked over and saw it was me as he says today "I saw the look in your eyes" and he hollered my name "Ralph" Don't do it man! I got you; I got you! And he took care of the debt. This time it was Ricky that was lucky, or was it? Ricky Hall RIP, can credit Skip Smith with saving his life that day.

Chapter 18

MY WITS END

In February 1994 I had had enough of the mistrust, deception, and quite frankly dysfunction with my girlfriend. I had been up for a matter of days getting high and so had she, but she had just gotten her public aid check. I was so agitated that morning that as I watched her across the street on the pay phone I decided that this was one day that I was going to get her, I was going to pay her back for all the deception that I felt that she had demonstrated over the years. So, I found the baseball bat and when she walked in the door I flew into a rage. I think that to this day she knew that her life was hanging in the balance. I grabbed her so she would not run and drew the bat back and screamed "you're going to die today" I demanded all of her money and she threw it on the ground at that moment one of my little children said, "Dad, don't kill my mama." I snapped out of it and let her go as she ran out the door. I picked up the money and exited the back door. I knew she was going to call the police, but I didn't care at that time... I was sick of her.

I ended up going to my oldest brother's house and using up all the money on drugs. He and his girlfriend were addicts as well but it was then that I realized that I had burned all my bridges and I had nowhere to go. I ended up sleeping on the floor of my brothers which was a smokehouse... I stayed there for about two days and nights when early Wednesday, February 9, 1994, I found myself walking down State Street with no destination in mind.

Chapter 19

The Dawn of a New Day

I remember thinking about what a mess I had made in my life and how I would give up a million dollars if I had it just for peace. A car pulled up while I was walking and thinking, it was a white lady with license plates on her car from Iowa, and she asked me if I knew where to find some dope. As I took around town looking for dope, we were pulled over by the police and I was arrested for a bench warrant for failure to appear and was put in the backseat of the police car. I had been there so many times before but this time it was different.

Supernatural Encounter With God

God knows how much we can bare, and God knew I was at my end. I remember sitting there and hearing God say to me "son you've tried everything else why don't you just try me" from that moment on, I began to see a vision of my life starting as a young child beginning as a dream of being an airline pilot and all the multiple stents in jail this time was different. I ended up staying in jail for three months.

I was in jail I was broken, empty, I was confused, hurt, and to the point that I thought that I would be better off dead. I knew that I needed a new life but I just didn't know where to start or what to do and eventually, I went to this young man's cell when no one else was there. Everybody hung around his cell because he was selling his commissary. When the crowd cleared out, we began to talk and he said to me, Hawthorne how are you? I said I'm fine but mind you I was a drug addict, I was really at the end of my rope, I was so sick and tired of being sick and tired, but I tried to fake it.

Anybody could tell that I was not in the best of shape, but he just looked at me and said, "no you're not, but you are going to be all right" immediately, tears begin to roll down my cheeks so I turned around so that nobody could see the tears and at that time the cell block was full to capacity, so I had to sleep on a mattress on the floor.

I was so hurt by the realization that I had let my life turn out the way that I did and now I had time to stop and breathe, but there was something about the young man and what he had said to me. When everyone left his cell, I went back in and asked him why did you say that to me, and he said, "I don't know, but God knows. I began to look around his cell, and he had the words "God loves you" written on the walls, and when I turned back to him, he said… "man, God loves you" It was like a well broke and I began to weep, and he began to share the gospel of Jesus Christ with me, and he began to tell me how he grew up in the church but had backslid and ended up on drugs and how he had rededicated his life to the Lord. He explained to me how he understood the foundation of the word, and he understood the plan of salvation. He shared that with me, and he told me how that *God so loved the world that he gave his only begotten son whosoever would believe in him should not perish but have eternal life.* John 3:16 and how that *if any man be in Christ he is a new creature old things are passed away behold all things become new 2 Corinthians 5:17* and how that if I repented of my sin and *Confess with my mouth and believe in my heart that Jesus died, He was buried, and He rose again for my sin that I would be saved. For with the heart man believeth unto righteousness; and the mouth confession is made unto salvation Romans 10:9-10* So, so, I confessed Jesus and that date was **February 9th, 1994**. I ask Him to come into my life and be my Savior.

The day that I made that commitment the very day that I allowed Jesus Christ to come into my life, my life changed forever. I started to go to chapel services and bible study once a week regularly. God's word began to grow in my heart, and I began to see clearly that all the challenges and situations that occurred in my life were not merely by chance. I found out that in the book of

Ephesians 6:10-12 [10] *Finally, my brethren, be strong in the Lord and in the power of His might.* [11] *Put on the whole armor of God, that you may be able to stand against the [] wiles of the devil.* [12] *For we do not wrestle against flesh and blood, but against principalities, against powers, against the rulers of [] the darkness of this age, against spiritual hosts of wickedness in the heavenly places.*

That verse of scripture transformed me and caused me to see that what the apostle Paul spoke about in Romans 7:14 was clearly what I was fighting, it reads; [14] *We know that the Law is right and good, but I am a person who does what is wrong and bad. I am not my own boss. Sin is my boss.*

You see *Romans 3:23 say that the wage of sin is death, but the gift of God is eternal life.*

I came to realize that the only way to rid myself of this situation was to let go of my old life and let Jesus be my Lord and Savior and then transform my mind according to

Romans 12:1-2 NLV *Christian brothers, I ask you from my heart to give your bodies to God because of His loving-kindness to us. Let your bodies be a living and holy gift given to God. He is pleased with this kind of gift. This is the true worship that you should give Him. ² Do not act like the sinful people of the world. Let God change your life. First, let Him give you a new mind. Then you will know what God wants you to do. And the things you do will be good and pleasing and perfect. You* see Proverbs 14:12NLV tells us that, *There is a way which looks right to a man, but its end is the way of death.*

I was a walking dead man and didn't even know it. So many of us go through our entire life thinking that we are in control, and in all actuality, we are not. Either God sits on the throne of our hearts or Satan. Look with me at *Deuteronomy 30:19 I call heaven and earth to speak against you today. I have put in front of you life and death, the good and the curse. So choose life so you and your children after you may live.*

To live this new life, you must first decide. That the decision you make will determine whether you live or die. (Spiritually and Naturally)

While in Jail my status changed after I was sentenced and they put me on as a trustee, so I ended up going to Bible studies at night where I saw a friend of mine from years back come in to teach the study, his name was Jonathan Byrd. It had been years since I had seen him. He had gone to prison on a 20 year sentence and he was out, his eyes were bright, he was spunky, and he looked fresh. I knew that he was a changed man. I don't know to this day what he taught that day because I was looking at the light shining off his life and I said to myself "God if you could do that for him you could do it for me" and He did it for me, he changed my life from the inside out. I began to speak to everyone I know in the jail about Jesus and tell them about the grace of God and how he had changed my life. Many did not believe me and laughed in my face. I got it, it sounded to them like another jailhouse conversion that never seemed to last. I stayed faithful to his word, and I read the Bible every day and the truth was being revealed to me. *John 8:32 NLV Then you will know the truth, and the truth will set you free."*

I called my girlfriend and started telling her about my experience, I would tell her that from this day forward "I'm looking forward and up" I would minister to her in ways that I never knew I could, and she gave her life to Christ and God delivered her from the drugs and alcohol and prostitution.

When I got out of jail as a part of my probation conditions, I was ordered to attend an extensive outpatient treatment program.

At that point in my life, I had been diagnosed by a psychiatrist as a chronic alcoholic and addict with an anti-social disorder. They said that that was my diagnosis, and I would be in that condition until I died. BUT GOD SAID, "NOT SO"

No one believed that as chronic of an addict as I was, I would be able to fulfill the requirements set before me by the courts to complete OUTPATIENT CARE successfully, but I did. Because little did everyone know I was already set free and delivered; achieving 9 months of outpatient treatment was but a stepping stone. I embraced it, *took what I could learn about addiction, and applied it to my life, but the scripture tells me in John 8:36 So if the Son sets you free, you will be free.*

My girlfriend became my wife; we had been dating in an addictive drug-induced and alcohol-fueled relationship for 11 years, but God delivered her and set her free as well, and we became husband-and-wife in August of 1994. We would study our bibles together and grow in God; we also studied for our GEDs because we both were high school dropouts. After acquiring our GEDs, we enrolled in college together. Leteena is a glowing light for us all and a major example for others to see that all things are possible with God.   I achieved all this while also attending OIC Vocational Institute, where I earned my certification in Child Development and attended NA meetings.

On the evening of my graduation from OIC, Executive Director Jessie Bates pulled me to the side and said that someone wanted to meet me after hearing of my continued success. His name was Dan Arnold. After speaking with him for a while, he gave me his card and told me to let him know if I ever needed anything. It turns out that Dan was a Christian who loved the Lord and God's people. As it turned out, he was a board member at OIC and somehow obtained my phone number and would call me weekly to ask how I was doing and if I needed anything.   It turned out that he was a man of many means and resources. He and I became very good friends, and he introduced me to Gideons International an organization that places the bible in hospitals, jails, and nursing homes. I met some of the most solid Christians in God's army there.

It is a love story that only God could write, and we are obliged to be the main subjects. He had done it when nothing else worked. I had been to three separate treatment centers over the years. I tried my will, I left town to only take my habit with me. You can run, but you can't hide from the sin of addiction. Luke 18:27 says: *And he said, the things that are impossible with man are possible with God.*

I am not writing about my life to glorify any of it. Frankly, the years I suffered from addiction were some of the darkest days of my life. I don't advise anyone to try anything I have written about other than Christ. I have been extremely blessed to come out of it all because I have many friends who were not as fortunate. What

God has done for me is that He took my mess and turned me into a messenger.

My brother Charles Hawthorne was a chronic addict as well, and a lot of addicts would go to his apartment to use, and he would get some of their dope in return. On our way to church many times, Leteena and I would stop in and pray and plead the blood of Jesus over that apartment and everybody in it. People would be hiding their dope and paraphernalia as we prayed for deliverance and healing.

My brother Robert was terminally Ill at the time and passed away not much longer. One day before he passed, some guys came to Charles's apartment and pistol-whipped him, and put a large gash in his head. After going to the hospital, even though Robert wanted to retaliate. Charles chose to come to my house instead. When he rang the doorbell, I answered, and he was standing there with a look on his face. I asked him, "You're ready, aren't you?" He just shook his head and said, yes, leteena and I prayed with him and he excepted Christ into his life that day and his life has not been the same since. Charles never returned to that old drug house and moved in with us, where he attended church and bible study on regular occasions. His estranged girlfriend, who was also an addict, began to watch us all as we grew in the Lord and stayed drug and alcohol-free. She eventually began to go to church with us and surrendered her life to Christ. Shortly afterward she and Charles were married, they are both currently ministers and head up their ministry called DC Restoring Hope. They are responsible for restoring hope through Jesus Christ to scores of individuals and families. PRAISE GOD!!!!!

in 1994 after my miraculous transformation, I was approached by an anointed woman of God while at a workshop name Sister Estella Benford. She said "son" I was sitting behind you and I heard the spirit of God tell me that you are the one that's supposed to help me fulfill the vision for a city-wide youth outreach ministry. I was amazed to see God's hand in my life again because I knew I should be working with youth. Sis Benford (may she RIP) and I, along with a few members of Deliverance Crusaders Church, which was under the leadership of Apostle Arnil Smith, began to do outreach, and I helped to launch the Let's Talk It Out, Not Act it Out Youth Outreach Ministry that I led as the Executive Director for ten years.

In 1999 I was licensed as a minister at St. Paul Church of God and Christ, in 2004 I was then ordained as an Elder under the leadership of Bishop James E. Washington who has been an inspiration in my personal life and ministry over the years. I served at St. Paul from 1999 until 2007, when Leteena and I relocated to Atlanta Ga. where we launched the Beyond the Walls Evangelistic Ministries in 2012. BTW as it's known, is a 501 3c tax-exempt organization. Leteena and I are currently worshipping God at the Church With Out Walls under the leadership of Pastor Ralph Douglas West in Houston Tx. where we have resided since 2015 after relocating from Atlanta.

I'm writing this book with the hopes that if you, the reader, have gone through anything in your life that you don't think God is willing to forgive you for that, you would have inspiration and motivation to know that what God has done in my life He can surely do in yours.

There is no low that God can't reach it is the sick that need a doctor. Jesus was known to interact with those counted out or not accepted in society because of what is believed to be unacceptable norms.

God looks beyond our faults and sees our needs. Our need is to be reconciled with Him. Matthew 6:33 says to seek ye first the kingdom of God, and his righteousness and all other things will be added to you.

I realized that I had a God-size hole in my heart that only God could fill. See, I searched high and low throughout my lifetime to find that one thing that would make me feel complete, to be made whole. I tried it all. Women, drugs, alcohol, partying, I am currently 29 years drug and alcohol-free, and Leteena and I have been a couple for almost 40 years. God is faithful even when we are not. WON'T HE DO IT?

Acknowledgments

I want to acknowledge my wonderful, talented, and anointed wife Leteena Teena Hawthorne for inspiring me to finish this piece of work when I didn't feel like I had it in me. Thank you Teena you are a great partner and certainly, a help mate that I am so blessed to have on my side.

Marathette Carroll has been pushing me and motivating me for years to do this; thank you my friend, for seeing in me what I didn't see in myself. I pray that you will be blessed with the work that our Lord has given me to complete.

To my nephew Johnie Blake, I wish you were here to celebrate this accomplishment with me, my greatest desire is to motivate you so that you will know that in spite of your situation, you can do all things through Christ who strengthens you.

In memory of my baby sister Lisa Lewis I wish that you were with us to celebrate this release of work with me, may you rest in peace and know that you are loved and missed.

In memory of my father and brother Robert Hawthorne and Robert Hawthorne Jr.

In memory of my mama Gillie Ree Haynes-Lewis

Made in the USA
Columbia, SC
11 February 2024

31802916R00038